EVERY DAY IS A NEW DAY

Every Day Is a New Day: A Story of Faith

Copyright© 2024 by Jenny Teeters
Published by Raven and Grace Press

ISBN Paperback: 9798990738607
ISBN Epub: 9798990738614

Printed in the United States of America
Designed by Jenny Teeters and Raven and Grace Press

For permission requests, contact the publisher at:
Raven and Grace Press
ravenandgrace.com
info@ravenandgrace.com

Visit https://jennyteeters.com/gift for a free guided meditation.

First Printing, 2024

EVERY DAY IS A NEW DAY

A Story of Faith

JENNY TEETERS, MBA

Raven + Grace

Raven and Grace Press

CONTENTS

Nine

Dedication

In profound gratitude and faith, I dedicate this work to God, who has shaped my journey and illuminated my path. May the words within these pages reflect the goodness and wisdom that flow from Him.

May these words resonate with the spirit of love, compassion, and hope that radiates from Jesus, St. Joseph, Mary Queen of Heaven, and my ever-watchful guardian angel.

I offer all my love and gratitude to Team Teeters who are my gifts from God.

I offer gratitude for the founders of the Twelve Steps and the trusted servants who have for almost a millennium, kept the doors open so that future addicts and alcoholics have a place to turn to and heal.

I offer gratitude for friends and family who believe in the power of prayer and prayed ceaselessly for me.

I love you so much Mommy, PJ, Sam, Trinity, Tsi, Lyle, Kristina, Garrett, Connor, Pam, Bill, Jack, Tommy, Stacy, Pat T., Phil, Jackie, Pat D., Dylan, Rebecca and Kenyon.

I offer gratitude for the Sisters Devoted to the Sacred Heart of Jesus for praying for me.

I offer gratitude to Catholic in Recovery and founder, Scott Weeman, who first introduced me to hope and healing through the Twelve Steps and the Sacraments.

Forewords

In *Every Day Is a New Day: A Story of Faith*, Jenny embarks on a profound odyssey of transformation and healing. Through the lens of the Twelve Steps and the sacramental life of the Church, Jenny unveils her journey from the depths of addiction to the heights of spiritual renewal. With unflinching honesty and vulnerability, she invites us to witness her struggles, doubts, and fears, reminding us that true healing begins with the courage to confront our brokenness.

This book is a testament to the redemptive power of God's love—a love both human and divine. Through personal stories and experience, we find how Jenny discovers a source of grace and renewal that sustains her on her journey toward sobriety and spiritual wholeness.

As we journey through these pages, may we be inspired by the resilience of the human spirit and the boundless mercy of God. May we find hope in despair, strength in adversity, and above all, may we discover that we are never alone—that a loving God walks beside us, guiding and loving us every step of the way.

I have been blessed to witness Jenny's re-birth and surrender to God as she found sobriety and new life. Once a puppet to the strings of alcohol and other addictions, Jenny now shares a riveting message of hope as a speaker, writer, trainer, personal coach, friend, mentor, and sponsor. The healing she's experienced has spilled into her family and enriched the lives of her daughters. Jenny's pathway to freedom is one that can encourage each of us to make positive changes today with the help of God.

Scott Weeman
Founder, Catholic in Recovery

As Jenny T's Executive Business Coach, friend, and co-spiritual traveler, I am honored to encourage all to join Jenny as she fights through years of denial and awakens from a highly functional addiction-controlled life to living the raw truth of every day's ups and downs.

It's a rare moment when you can't put a book down – when you look forward to turning the next page after page to hear more about Jenny's struggles to refuse what could have been a lesser-addiction fueled life to most importantly following her role-modeled guidance about how others might choose and sustain sobriety.

This book is a guide for you, a loved one, a neighbor, a coworker, or perhaps someone you have noticed who needs to address denial and move beyond the addiction of choice. Through Jenny's trans-formational and highly personal journey, the recovery fight may start or be reinforced as you read through these pages of pain, honesty, hard work, and spiritual guidance.

This book will remind you that there is hope, help, and healing – that life can and will get better perhaps simply by beginning with this book.

Darlene Chambers, Ph.D.
Integrative Wellness Coach, Author of *I'm Just a Country Song: Three Chords and Only My Truth.*

Introduction

"The Spirit of the Lord is on me, because he has anointed me to proclaim good news to the poor. He has sent me to proclaim freedom for the prisoners and recovery of sight for the blind, to set the oppressed free. (Luke 4:18)

Let us begin with who I am and why I have something to say. Who am I?

I could answer that I'm Jenny T. I'm a wife and mother. I'm a sister, aunt, daughter, niece, cousin, and friend. I'm a corporate professional. I'm the founder and CEO of my own company. I'm a teacher. I'm a writer. I'm a volunteer. I'm a coach. I'm a mentor.

In the not too distant past, the answer to that question would be that I am a liar.

I was living a lie every day. Those days turned into years. I was playing a role. I was presenting myself to the world in one way and concealing my addictive behaviors when I thought no one was looking.

I lived in a self-destructive prison, killing myself progressively day by day, week by week, and year by year. My self-destructive patterns hurt my husband, Steve, our marriage, our daughters Cordelia and Arabella, my mother, my siblings, my friends, strangers, my colleagues, my employer, my God, and myself.

I struggled with the fear of being unloved and unworthy of love. I had the fear of being rejected and not belonging. I protected myself at great cost to become a chameleon and carefully change before your eyes, constantly seeking and sensing what I should be saying, wearing, doing, and thinking. I protected myself by becoming financially indispensable to my family, through contributions in my community, and efforts to my employers.

I am a recovered meth and nicotine addict, recovered anorexic, recovering binge and restrictive eater, recovering alcoholic, recovering perfectionist, and recovering codependent. I also struggle with over-achievement and people-pleasing.

My drug of choice is alcohol, and this book is about God leading me and saving me from alcoholism, which if left untreated leads to death. It was leading me to my death.

My life has changed, and I am changed.

Today my answer to the question 'Who am I'?' is I am a beloved daughter of God. I am a channel of God's peace and a light in this world to amplify His light, love, and hope to His suffering children.

One of my favorite songs is "The Summons", and a line in the song is to 'Set my prisoners free'.

My intention in telling my story is to bring hope and understanding to you and your suffering friends and family, and to help set God's prisoners free. As I tell my story, I demystify the Twelve Steps and give a glimpse into transitioning from a life of disaster to a life in recovery.

For me, the transition was terrifying, and I had to be willing for a lifelong commitment and complete honesty about who I am – the best and the worst of me.

I was petrified by the unknown, and not getting help sooner built a mountain of regret and remorse. Heaps and heaps of regret and remorse.

I pray something I write will save you or a loved one and give you inspiration to seek where faith can set you free from any prison you are in.

Take a look at a day in the life of my alcoholism.

CHAPTER ONE

The Day I Was Almost Caught

I woke up at five in the morning determined to get to the gym.

I had been gaining weight at an alarming rate and no number of points or calorie counting (from food) was making a difference. Diet plans and workouts were no match for the number of calories I was consuming from alcohol.

I had a shot of green apple vodka from the freezer. And I had a second one.

I drove to the gym, completed my workout, and drove home.

I showered and got ready for the day. I had another shot.

I was going to carpool with coworkers to Silicon Valley a few hours away, so the fear was beginning to creep in of when my next drink would come and how many hours away the evening drinks would be.

I had another shot. And another one.

I left home to drive 30 minutes to meet my colleagues at an agreed upon meeting point.

As I exited the freeway in the rain, I reached for the directions, which I had printed and had fallen to the floor of the passenger side of the car. I took my eyes off the road for a moment to grab the directions and as I looked up to the road, I realized I had veered out of the lane.

I braked hard to correct, which sent me swerving and crashing through a fence on the onramp.

Time stopped for me at that moment. In slow motion, my airbag deployed as my car nosedived into a ditch.

Oh NO!!!

I am going to be in trouble. I am going to be late for my meeting and late for meeting my coworkers.

I called my husband to tell him I was in an accident and okay but needed a ride to my coworkers. He packed our little girls into the car to come to me.

A good Samaritan woman saw the accident and pulled over. She asked if I was okay, and she said she called the police.

Oh NO!!! I wanted to turn back time.

Not to take back the shots but to take back the accident.

My heart was pounding as I grabbed my briefcase and purse and pulled myself out of the ditch in my business suit. I waited for what was to come next.

A police officer arrived to find me standing with my briefcase next to my car nose-first in the ditch and completely totaled.

He asked about my safety and told me that he wasn't sure if it was my perfume or hair spray, but he thought he smelled alcohol.

He walked me to his car and ran me through several tests on my fingers. He asked me to close my eyes and stand on one foot. Then he asked for a number of other motor skills tests, and he seemed agitated that I was passing them.

The officer also asked me when I had my last drink and I said the night before, but I didn't remember the time because I told him honestly that I didn't remember. I had a blackout the night before so I didn't remember when I went to bed.

There I stood in heels. The wind was blowing through my long blonde hair. Arms outstretched and following his every direction with precision.

I could see my husband and daughters parked in the distance as he asked me to have a seat in the back of his car to look up my driver's license.

I was terrified. It was the first time I had ever been asked to sit in the back seat of a patrol car.

The officer was frustrated that he did not have a breathalyzer with him. I had passed the roadside assessment and he had to let me go. I was driven to Steve and the girls, and Steve drove me to my coworkers who were waiting for me and very worried.

I communicated I was just fine, and we sped to the ever important meeting, which was a success.

By the time I got home, the only thing I wanted was a drink. Ten drinks. Twenty drinks.

Enough drinks to make the memories of the day fade away.

The next day I woke up and had a shot of vodka first thing in the morning to start my cycle of another insane alcoholic day.

Reflect & Write: Take a moment to journal about how this section resonates with you. Share your reflections with someone close to you.

CHAPTER TWO

A Vision of What Is Possible

At the time of writing this book, I am sixty days abstinent from flour and sugar. I am four years sober from alcohol. I am twenty-seven years clean from methamphetamine. I am twenty-four years abstinent from tobacco.

I have a gratitude practice every day where I text my sponsor at least three things I am grateful for. This practice has grown where I also exchange daily gratitude lists with family, friends, and my mommy.

Some of the most beautiful fruits of my life today are:

- I have compassion and understanding for my fellows in recovery whether they are struggling with food, sex, technology, drugs, alcohol, control, pornography, work, anger, success, attention, and any number of the other addictions and unhealthy attachments.
- I don't judge others harshly because I understand that addictions bring us to terrible consequences, including imprison-

ment, loss of family, loss of friends, loss of home, loss of self-dignity, and feelings of worthlessness.

- My family and friends trust me.
- I savor nature, quiet, peace, and serenity.
- I have received a calling and no longer wonder 'Is this all there is to life?'
- I have unlimited opportunities to be creative and use my talents.
- I have physically healed and have the desire to move my body and eat nutritious foods.
- I have forgiven myself for all that I have done, and I have been forgiven completely by God and by most friends and family.
- I feel at ease in my own skin and happy with my essence and my soul.
- My children have been a part of my recovery and have no shame or fear of asking for help and communicating their needs.
- I am a force for good in this world.
- I have remained willing each day to do what it takes to stay clean and sober.
- I am willing to practice receiving unlimited love from my husband.
- I set boundaries.
- I ask myself the question and seek warning signs of 'Am I trying to please someone out of fear?'
- I have a healthy, fun, and loving marriage.

Reflect & Write: Take a moment to journal about how this section resonates with you. If you were to declare an obstacle in your life, what would it be and how would you like your life to be different?

CHAPTER THREE

How This Book Is Organized

God has led me through an incredible journey of transformation. What was wrong has been made right, and God has healed me with His love and mercy.

I am going to share my story with you about a tradition that I was taught in Twelve Step fellowship groups.

I am going to share with you:

- Part I: What life was like
- Part II: What happened
- Part III: Willingness
- Part IV: Working the Twelve Steps
- Part V: What life is like now

We are going to cover some of my early life, early indicators of my addictive nature, and Divine inspiration or seeds that were planted in me early by God, which led me to recovery.

I recommend you read this book as a narrative story. You can skip around, but as a quote from one of our family's favorite movies, *Pitch Perfect*, "It really builds."

I have blended where God has led me and protected me throughout my journey, the progression of my disease, and the very special gifts I received from fellows on my journey.

I am going to share how God divinely has guided my life, how He set this prisoner free, and how God did for me what I could not do for myself.

I will share scripture passages and prayers throughout the book and what they mean to me.

I am going to share how every day is a new day through this story of faith.

As you journey with me throughout this book, I will engage you frequently to reflect, journal, and respond with your own story. I recommend you have a laptop, journal, or notepad nearby for your self-discovery responses.

FIVE-MINUTE REFLECTIONS are placed throughout this book as a space for you to have a few moments of mindfulness with your reactions, own experiences, and responses to what you have read. I invite you to take a few breaths to notice your thoughts and feelings before beginning to write.

You will also find **Reflect & Write** sections where you can take notes and answer guided questions about what you are going through in your own life.

CHAPTER FOUR

My Hope for You

My hope for you as you read this story is that you find inspiration that the obstacles, addictions, and unhealthy attachments you have, or your loved one has, DO have a solution and that millions of people who have been healed can show you and be with you on your journey of recovery.

Where you are completely without hope, I will show you how to turn around hopelessness and helplessness.

Oh, I know that you are suffering. You may be suffering yourself or suffering for a loved one.

We don't have to look far to find someone in need of help from the dangers of overdoing or being overly controlling and restrictive.

I know that you might be hiding. I know that you might feel shame, regret, remorse, and anger. I know that you might be in denial. I know that you might be at a loss for where to go next. I know that your family is praying for you. Your friends are praying for you. I pray for you every day. Twelve Step programs pray for you to find them.

God wants to answer your prayers.

I know that God is pursuing you and will never give up on you. He will allow you your willfulness and when that willfulness turns to willingness to heal, His Grace will shower you and completely turn your life around.

If this is a family member or friend of someone who is dealing with addiction or unhealthy attachments, I know you wish you could say the right words, pray the right prayers, or make the right calls to help someone in your life. You may have spent money over and over for someone. Or set them up with jobs, shelter, and opportunities, and it is unfathomable as to why they cannot change.

My hope with this story is that you see that healing, love, and forgiveness are possible.

Reflect & Write: Take a moment to journal about how this section resonates with you. What is your prayer for yourself or a loved one?

CHAPTER FIVE

PART I: What Life Was Like

Addicted to Attention and People Pleasing

One of the best exercises I learned to do and help others with when achieving my coaching certification was to take a 'step back'.

Step back. Step back and look back. Step back and see connections. Step back and see the big picture.

I'll take a step back here into some early memories that highlight some of my behaviors and characteristics, which led me on a self-pity path to self-destruction.

I heard a sobriety sister speak honestly one day about being addicted to attention, which led her to her drug and alcohol addiction into the sex trade.

I could completely relate to gaining male attention for self-validation and trying to fill my need for belonging.

Now I will step back to kindergarten. I can remember at five years old standing outside at recess at a new school with no friends yet. I was watching a group of boys chase around a pretty girl with long shiny hair. Her two ponytails were gathered by old-fashioned hair ties that had red marbles on them. They were ruby red and shiny like her hair. The boys chased her and tickled her.

I remember distinctly thinking, I want to be that girl. I wanted that attention.

I remember asking the boys to chase me and tickle me and they did. It was awesome.

It was not long after that I began looking at my mom's romance novels. At an aunt's house, my older cousins read *Sweet Valley High* romance novels. At ages eight through ten, I began to build this picture in my mind of romance, popularity, love, family, and sex.

I avidly read romance novels and I also love romantic comedies. I paid close attention to what was on TV and that the pretty girls always got the attention. I also was aware of the shows that were on in the background growing up: *Little House on the Prairie, The Waltons, Leave it to Beaver, Andy Griffith, I Love Lucy, Happy Days, WKRP in Cincinnati*, and I charted my course.

I wanted to be very popular. I wanted a boyfriend and romance. I would get married young like my mother and grandmothers. I would have many children. I would have friend groups and entertain. I would have breakfast, lunch, and dinner on the table for my family and keep a neat house. Our extended family would all interact with our large family, and weekends and holidays would always be grand reunions. We'd be best friends with our neighbors, and all have so many barbecues, trips, potlucks, and holidays together. I would be loved, and I would belong. I would be safe.

What I didn't take into consideration was that what I was watching on TV was fiction. I was reading fiction. I was building an idea in my head of marriage and my future based upon fiction.

The only truth was that my father being one of seventeen children, and I being the second of five children, and my aunts and uncles also having large families, we did spend a lot of time together. My maiden name is Stewart and there are a great many Stewarts.

As a large Catholic family, we spent time together in many Masses, weddings, births, baptisms, summers, breaking bread, and holidays with grandparents, aunts, uncles, and dozens of cousins. I love it so much. My cousins felt like siblings that just didn't live in the same house as us. This was my community and where I felt so much love and belonging.

When I was ten, our family moved away from the cluster of Stewarts in central California to Sacramento. Although we visited frequently for the first few years after the move, there was a family rift I still don't fully understand and my father decided to cut ties to his family. My dad's decision also cut me off from an important source of love and belonging.

It was in Sacramento I started my fourth school, which was a Catholic K-8 school. The school was St. Lawrence and there was one class for every grade. Sixth through eighth grades for me had an average of fifteen students, and these students had been together for years. I was painstakingly aware that my clothes did not match the clothes of the popular girls. We did not have a lot of money when we got to Sacramento. My parents worked many jobs and many hours to provide for our needs and there was not much money left over for wants. It was going to take money to pay for Reebok high tops, feathered haircuts, and whatever else the other girls were wearing.

I could see the hierarchy of popularity in the class and I was landing second to last.

When I turned twelve and entered seventh grade, my parents allowed me to use makeup. I have loved makeup since I was a child and helped my mom unpack her boxes of Mary Kay cosmetics when she was a consultant.

We weren't allowed to wear makeup at school, and I was convinced I was not pretty without it on. After one summer, I returned to school in eighth grade with a full face of makeup. Each day I gradually removed a layer. One day no foundation. The next day no eye shadow. The next day no mascara.

A boy who sat in front of me turned around and looked me in the eye and said, "Every day you are getting uglier and uglier."

I suppose you can guess that I still love makeup and carry with me the shadow that I am ugly without.

One summer, a brother and I were snooping around in the garage and came across a briefcase full of *Playboy* magazines. I remember looking through those magazines and making a connection in my mind.

Men like women who look and act like that. If I look and act like that, men will like me.

I didn't know then about objectifying women, but I began to treat myself and allow others to treat me like an object.

I'll summarize that my behavior in high school and into my twenties remained attention seeking, and I was very promiscuous. I had no concept of self-dignity. I equated physical attention to acceptance. This resulted in teenage pregnancies and the decision to hide and conceal the consequences of my behavior by terminating those pregnancies.

I eventually found myself with a boyfriend who did drugs. And dealt drugs. I was with him for almost a year before I even knew as I'd never been around drugs.

One day he asked me if I wanted to try it and I said yes. He poured white powder into a glass of water, and I drank it. I was hooked.

This boyfriend experienced a tragic accident. For months he was in another state in intensive care before moving into his mother's home for long-term care. He suffered permanent brain damage from his accident.

After my boyfriend's tragic accident, I found myself from time to time hanging out with his friends. They thought I looked 'classy' for someone who did meth because I had a full-time job at the time and dressed in business attire. How in the world did I find myself at construction sites at night smoking meth? How did I find myself booking hotel rooms with one of those friends and trading my body for drugs?

Well, methamphetamine was engineered to be extremely powerful, and it blasted my body and brain with an amount of pleasurable sensations that I had never felt before. It is pure evil.

I'm extremely lucky that the person who provided the drugs lived out of town and stopped coming to Sacramento. My supply was thus cut off, and I was 'clean' but an untreated addict.

You can imagine this same misdirected instinct drove me to seek attention as I grew into womanhood.

My mother and grandmothers started their families in their late teens, and by the time I was twenty with no husband in sight I was feeling way behind schedule. I dated a lot of men. A lot. Sometimes many at the same time.

I met my husband at a wedding in the late nineteen hundreds. (I think it's funny to say late nineteen hundreds). He was the best man of the groom. I was a bridesmaid. His name is Steve. At the wedding, he gave a terrific speech. I was currently an instructor at an IT company, and I admired Steve's public speaking confidence, timing, humor, and how well the speech was crafted. He noticed me and told the groom he thought I looked spectacular in my bridesmaid dress. Spectacular was a larger vocabulary word than the words most of the men I dated used, and I agreed to give Steve my phone number.

Our first date was a double date with our newlywed friends. At the end of the date, Steve kissed me on the cheek and drove away. I was stunned. I thought perhaps he had no game. And I also thought perhaps I was being respected. That was a first for me. It was quite a shock.

I told Steve that I was dating several people and he told me that if I was dating other people, I would not be dating him. Once again, I was taken aback.

Not only did Steve show me respect, but he respected himself.

I called up these other fellows, told them that I had a new boyfriend and severed contact.

Getting back to my insatiable need for attention, I remember after a few years of marriage there was one afternoon I pranced around in front of Steve, happy to have lost some weight, and he said in slight frustration, "Who knew you were going to need this much attention?"

I knew that I would.

Before writing this book, I told my daughters about my history, my actions, and the consequences. I didn't want them to be surprised by my story. My husband knew about my past before we were married. I told my daughters individually and they held my hands and hugged me. The only question that they asked me was if I had forgiven myself. My daughters wanted that for me the most. At the time they asked, I could not honestly answer yes.

You'll find a few resources at the end of this book I found helpful in delving into how to heal, how to love myself, childhood trauma, self-image, body image, and self-esteem.

The Progression of My Disease

My parents did not drink daily, weekly, monthly, or yearly. I can recall only a few times that they drank. I remember once they had champagne at a wedding reception and took a nap when we got home. They also had gotten five children ready for a wedding, through a wedding, and home from a wedding.

As I was saying, my parents didn't drink often, but they did have a box with liquor in it that sat on the bottom of the pantry Lilyvale Court kitchen in Citrus Heights year after year. The box remained largely untouched until I was about sixteen years old. A friend in high school was helping me with my search for a boyfriend and introduced me to a man (not boy) who was going to come over.

I thought it would be very adult and impressive of me to offer him something to drink so I mixed some grenadine, gin, brandy, and other spirits together and offered it to him and drank some myself. I remember him turning it down after a few sips, but his cheeks turned bright red. I remember finishing the full plastic glass, and as I walked around the house, the floor seemed to be moving and I had a dizzy feeling. I *really* liked that feeling.

The next time I got drunk was after high school at a party my boyfriend had invited me to. Yes! I eventually landed a boyfriend. At this party everyone was playing a drinking card game, which I didn't understand the rules of, but I learned quickly that I wanted to lose at the game because that meant I could drink. I loved it! I remember playing that game and I remembered nothing else until the morning. My boyfriend was quite angry with me and embarrassed as he described me crawling around on the floor the rest of the game trying to go down on him in front of everyone. I think he eventually made me leave the game and put me to bed.

This disease is progressive so when I was in my twenties, drinking looked like this:

- Go to the bar with friends and drink dollar beers hours before anyone else and drink until I run out of money.
- Go to parties with friends and drink until someone made me leave - I had a lot of frustrated girlfriend babysitters.

- Go dancing with my sister and drink until the bar closes and she had to force me not to go to whatever after party I was being invited to by strangers.

During my marriage drinking looked like this:

- Alcohol in the house! Alleluia.
- Drinking by the pool on the weekends and every night
- Starting my weeknight drinking the moment I got home until bedtime
- Embarrassing my husband at every wedding, party, and event
- Being babysat during every girls trip
- Day drinking on weekends
- Remote work begins and I drink before stressful meetings
- I begin day drinking no matter what kind of meetings I'm having
- Hiding how much I'm drinking and going to various stores to buy the volume of alcohol I needed
- Tension, confusion, pleading, and an eventual detachment as our marriage eroded
- Trying to control drinking: only drink on weekends, only drink with meal-plan points, only drink beer and wine, only drink when eating out, don't have alcohol in the house, bring alcohol back into the house to save money from paying for it outside of the house ... and on and on.
- Going to counseling to find out why I am so miserable
- Abruptly departing from counseling when Alcoholics Anonymous (AA) pamphlets are offered to me
- Ultimately drinking one bottle of vodka a day on average from the moment I woke up, all day, into the evening, until I fell asleep or blacked out. If I woke up in the night, had a drink to

go back to sleep, stayed intoxicated twenty-four hours a day for years.

Throughout my disease's progression, I was a high-functioning alcoholic, so I was able to work full time, get promoted, get stock options, and get bonuses - until I lost my job.

I was able to run marathons until I couldn't hide that I needed to drink before, during, and after a run.

I was able to teach fitness classes until I drank before class and injured myself.

I was able to function on leadership boards and in the community until I started to miss commitments because I couldn't drive safely to and from them.

I was able to socialize until I was an embarrassment, and the invitations stopped coming and I abandoned my friendships for alcohol.

I was able to participate in my family's life until I blacked out so often, I could hardly remember conversations that happened during the day.

I was able to look relatively healthy until I swelled to almost 230 pounds. My eyes turned yellow, I vomited daily, bled when I had bowel movements, had insomnia, dry heaved, passed out, got dizzy often, stopped regularly brushing and flossing my teeth, wore less makeup, and had lapses in my memory.

I had a zest for life until the disease took over, and drink by drink, I stopped living and was speeding towards death.

And then God intervened again and introduced someone into my life who changed the course of self-destruction completely.

Reflect & Write: Take a moment to journal about how this section resonates with you. Do you notice any progression of your behaviors?

CHAPTER SIX

PART II: What Happened

ONE IMPORTANT LIFE EVENT THAT IMPACTED ME IN A WAY I NEVER IMAGINED WAS WHEN MY FATHER PASSED AWAY. HE WAS DIAGNOSED WITH MELANOMA AND FOUGHT FOR A VERY LONG TIME UNTIL THE CANCER TOOK HIM AT AGE 59.

I learned years later that unresolved emotional issues with a parent can complicate the grieving process. I was overwhelmed with the loss, saddened for the rest of our very large immediate and extended family, and often still angry at situations from the past. I didn't know how to channel any of the feelings.

I planned and organized in a haze right after his passing, enrolled in an Executive MBA program, and for many months worked a full-time corporate job, taught Zumba, participated in the graduate program, and drank my feelings away when there was any break in the business.

Through the years of my dad's treatments, I found myself going back to Mass at Our Lady of the Assumption in Carmichael, California. After my dad passed, I remember going to church one day, sitting in the pew, and reading in the bulletin that they were accepting applications for the Pastoral Council. I didn't know what the Pastoral Council was, but I was interested in applying.

I also would be in Mass and have an impulse or idea that I could help like the other parishioners I saw lecturing and volunteering. In a short time, I became part of the Pastoral Council, a Lector and Eucharistic Minister. I also began helping with communications and other committees. I found peace at Our Lady of the Assumption where I could not find it anywhere else.

The Pastoral Council had scheduled a retreat in 2018, and I attended the retreat listening to a variety of presenters. I listened to a young man, named Scott, give a talk on Catholic in Recovery. He started his talk introducing himself as a Child of God. I didn't know anything about how to identify myself like he did, nor about recovery, but bought his book and accepted an invitation to dinner with the Pastoral Council president and Scott that evening. It was during that dinner that I became aware that the church wanted to start Catholic in Recovery meetings, and I was asked to lead the meetings.

It was surprising since I didn't know anything about recovery, and I remember looking into Scott's eyes and saying, "I don't know anything about the Twelve Steps."

He looked into my eyes and paused and said, "You are going to."

I had confidence that I could facilitate any subject matter once becoming familiar with it, so we decided on the day of the week and time that meetings would begin.

Little did I know that I would indeed learn to recite the Twelve Steps, and eventually I would pray to them over and over begging for God's help.

Catholic in Recovery representatives held, and hold, virtual meetings and in-person meetings in many parts of the world daily. It was during these meetings that I would learn the format and how to lead the meetings at Our Lady of the Assumption.

The men and women who came to the meeting I facilitated were struggling with many addictions and unhealthy attachments. Many were clean and sober for decades and were part of other Twelve Step fellowships. Some people were dealing with food. Some people were dealing with sex and pornography. Some people were desperate to help a loved one with an addiction. It was in these meetings I met people for the first time who had been addicted and were no longer suffering. They came together regularly to share and explain that Catholic in Recovery was offering a space to be openly Catholic in their recovery.

I had not been to any other Twelve Step recovery meetings, so I didn't quite understand why Catholic in Recovery was so refreshing to them and freeing for them. I was hiding my alcoholism from everyone and regularly facilitated the meetings intoxicated.

God had put everything in my path that I needed to surrender.

I had lost my job, so I had nothing but time on my hands, which had made my drinking worse and my desperation stronger. Every physical symptom was getting worse and I was completely hopeless.

It was on November 12, 2019, that I received the gift of desperation and completely surrendered myself to God.

It was another night of insomnia. I always saved enough alcohol to get through the morning shakes, so I knew I couldn't drink anymore, which was causing me a terrible amount of distress. I left the bedroom frustrated with tossing and turning and went to the couch.

I tried to fall asleep on the couch, but I couldn't. I started to cry. I let the fear, shame, humiliation, defeat, anxiety, stress, lack of character, failure all rise and I began to pray fervently. I prayed to my grandmothers I had lost. I prayed to my father. I prayed to my grandfathers I had lost. I prayed to my aunts and uncles. I prayed to the babies I knew were in heaven. I prayed to Jesus. I prayed to Mary. I prayed to Joseph. I prayed to all the saints collectively. I prayed to all the angels.

I sobbed and prayed that I was powerless over alcohol and that my life was unmanageable - Step 1. I prayed that only a power greater than myself could restore me to sanity - Step 2. I prayed and gave my will and my life over to the care of God as I understood him - Step 3.

I begged and prayed for Step 1, Step 2, and Step 3 over and over until I eventually went to sleep.

The next morning when I woke up, I needed alcohol. I went to the hiding spot with a clear glass and poured the small amount that I had saved from the night before. I went into the kitchen to mix it with juice or water flavoring like I had done hundreds of mornings before. I paused at the sink, and I poured the very last of the alcohol that I had down the sink. I went back to bed.

Never with my own willpower had I been able to run out of or dispose of alcohol.

So if the Son sets you free, you will be free indeed.
(John 8:36)

And then I got *very* sick. It was not a smart thing to do. Stopping completely after having consumed so much alcohol every day for years. I was shaking. I couldn't keep anything down - not even water. I told my family I must have caught a cold or flu or food poisoning because I was in terrible shape. I slept in and out of the shakes and sweats. I heard whispers and had nightmares, which were terrifying.

My husband kept coming to me asking what I thought had happened. He was baffled and I was unwilling to be honest.

I made it through twenty-four hours.

On the second morning I was starting to feel a little better, and I went into the kitchen to get some water. My husband was staring blankly at his laptop. Even through watching me change over time and having no idea how I had come to look and behave so unhealthily, he was usually a jovial and talkative person.

Not that morning. That morning, he was lifeless. He said that he was experiencing depression.

I tried to go for a moment of honesty and I told him I was experiencing depression, too.

He pointed at me and he said, "I am experiencing depression because of you."

He went to work and I made a decision to tell him when he came home what was happening. I don't remember much of the day as I stayed in bed again. I remember texting the Catholic in Recovery group members and telling them that I had been lying to them for the months I had been leading the group. I said that I was going to tell my husband what was happening to me and I may not be married anymore by the evening time.

They sent a flood of prayers my way and a warning. Under no circumstances have a drink. I was on day two of sobriety and I could make it to day three.

When my husband came home, I asked him to come to our room. I closed the door and I sat on the bed. I could not look him in the eye.

I told him, "I am an alcoholic and I am having withdrawal symptoms. I have been hiding how much I have been drinking from you for many years, and I need to go to the doctor. I need to go to AA and I need a sponsor."

My husband gave me a big hug, which I did not expect at all. He said, "Let's go and tell the girls."

We walked together to the kitchen and I told the girls the same thing. The three of them had no idea. They stared at me and were loving. I had shocked them all with the truth. I had shocked myself by telling the truth.

My life began to change from that moment forward. God had kept me sober and I was still married that night. The first of many miracles were beginning to happen in my life.

Reflect & Write: Take a moment to journal about how this section resonates with you. Do you have a secret that is making you sick either physically or spiritually?

CHAPTER SEVEN

PART III: Willingness

Courage and Willingness

With only a few days of sobriety, feeling physically sick, spiritually ashamed, and scared, I went to see my doctor. I had been avoiding my doctor for years and when I told him that I am an alcoholic, how much I had been drinking every day, how I stopped, and physically how I was feeling, he expressed tremendous compassion.

My doctor told me he wished I had called him because he could have eased the withdrawal process with medicine. He told me that now I was sober, I should remember to communicate adult to adult and as equals with my husband. Although I was sick, it was not appropriate for me to accept a parent-child relationship with my husband or with anyone. He also interestingly told me I wasn't required to share every thought I had with anyone.

I believe my doctor had personal experience and wisdom he was passing along to me.

I asked my doctor what he recommended as next steps because my husband was skeptical of Alcoholics Anonymous, but he trusted our doctor. My doctor offered to refer me to a substance abuse program.

I will always remember my doctor for treating me gently as an ill person and without judgment.

Treatment Program

I was nervous as I went to my intake appointment at the hospital. I filled out a questionnaire and answered a series of questions. The intake coordinator told me that they had an inpatient and out-patient option, and he recommended by my interview that I enroll in the outpatient program. The program was for one year. The program had four phases, and during the first phase there would be a requirement to attend at least three Twelve Step fellowship meetings and that I would provide urine regularly, which would be tested for drugs and alcohol.

My Mommy

My husband was very nervous in the beginning leaving me alone at home, especially the first few days. I had broken all trust and he didn't trust me not to get alcohol. When a grocery store trip was needed, he asked our children to accompany me. I am proud of our girls for telling him no and communicating that they did not want the job of being my guards.

During the first couple of weeks of sobriety, I would take the girls to school and I would go to my mom's house. My mom lovingly made me food I could stomach, and I helped her pack for moving out of her home. She was renting a home for the second time since my dad's passing and the owners were selling.

I LOVE my mommy.

As each day went on, I felt physically better and was in awe of the miracle of several days in a row of not drinking after I had been such a slave to alcohol.

I had my first trigger at my mom's house as we were in her kitchen cleaning out cabinets. I noticed that she had a full bottle of vodka in the cabinet. My first instinct was to imagine how to get into it if she went to the restroom or left to get the mail. I was so distracted while she was talking to me, I could hardly concentrate on her words. I was obsessed and told her that I needed to leave. By the grace of God, that proximity to alcohol did not tempt me to pause at a store and drink. God helped me in that moment and the moment passed.

Twelve Step Meetings

I went to my first Twelve Step meeting when I was eight days sober. I was still green around the gills, swollen, ashamed, terrified, and it took a lot of courage to walk into the room. I walked in and zeroed in on an empty seat next to someone with a binder. I felt like the first day of school and had a notepad, pen, and water. I sat up straight and was ready to learn. I had my slip with me, which I needed someone to sign to prove I had attended the meeting.

Everyone was very gentle with me and shared what to say when a basket was passed for my slip to be signed.

"I'm Jenny, and I'm an alcoholic."

People had such encouraging smiles on their faces when I said those embarrassing words. Afterwards I was surrounded by ladies offering a list of phone numbers, introducing themselves, asking if I'd ever tried to be sober before, asking if it was my first meeting, and asking if I had a sponsor.

At the second meeting I went to one of the Twelve Step members had a stack of books with him and offered them to the group as he got them from a garage sale. I asked for one of the books that day.

The third meeting the ladies came to me again asking if I had a sponsor, and one woman in particular was looking me directly in the eyes. I tried to give this woman my business card to call me and chat about being my sponsor. She stared at the card and told me that isn't exactly how it worked. She told me that I could take her phone number and call her. She also told me if I wanted a sponsor, I would need to ask the question. Meep! To pick up the phone and ask someone for help was uncomfortable for me. It would be taking a risk of potential rejection.

I'd made it through the second week sober. I made it through three Twelve Step meetings, and I made it through one week of outpatient rehab.

I did call and ask this woman to be my sponsor and she said yes. She told me exactly what she expected and how she and I were going to work together. I'll share more in the next section of the book.

My routine was to get up and get ready, take the girls to school, go to outpatient rehab, come home for lunch, and light a candle and say the St. Joseph Holy Cloak novena and cry my eyes out, go to my Twelve Step meeting, get the girls from school, prepare dinner, and wait in the awkward silence of the house for the next day to come and repeat the process.

Therapy

Part of the outpatient rehab was to have a therapist and weekly appointments. I had tried therapy a few times, but when inevitable questions of how much I was drinking came up I lied and stopped going. One therapist helped me cope a little with the burning shame from the experience of incest in my past, but the day she passed me an Alcoholics Anonymous pamphlet I knew I was caught and I did not go back to her. I had been more concerned with a good grade from past therapists and my image than I was with being honest and finding healing.

This time was different and I met a woman who doled out tough love to me. I didn't realize yet that my illness is terminal. It is a death sentence, and my therapist and the entire curriculum of the outpatient program ensured that it was completely understood. My denial at my impact on my family and excuses for drinking were addressed. That I had made my spouse my higher power and resented him for it. My self-will, self-seeking, and selfish behaviors were revealed. My true understanding of the verbal and emotional abuse I was experiencing from my boss was revealed, and my therapist helped me create an action plan to remove myself from the relationship. I was honest and received my therapist's feedback willingly, although looking at myself honestly was unfamiliar. I had many villains in my life, but up until that point I had not taken accountability as the No. 1 offender.

Marriage

Communication was tense in the house as the cycle everyone had been operating around my drinking was turned upside down by the truth. I was sober, I was present, and my husband was understandably angry and confused. COVID-19 had struck at this time, and I wasn't employed so I would join him on neighborhood dog walks. We'd see so many neighbors who he knew and communicated with. He'd talk about himself and *his* girls, and I would stand there realizing I had been invisible in the picture for so long that he wasn't used to us being a couple or presenting ourselves as a married unit any longer.

At this point we had been married twenty years. We did not talk of a separation but there was no talk about a future either. I was uncertain day to day where we were headed as a married couple.

Reflect & Write: Take a moment to journal about how this section resonates with you. If you were to surround yourself with a supportive team, what would that look like?

CHAPTER EIGHT

PART IV: Working the Twelve Steps

There are many Twelve Step programs, and it is my experience that the steps themselves remain the same as does the tradition of one person who has been through the steps is then encouraged and accountable to help the next person receive what they were freely given.

I was confused about what qualified someone to be a sponsor and asked around if there was a class or certification program people took to prepare and receive a credential. If you know me, you are probably smiling because my background is in developing training programs and certifications, thus this line of questioning seemed reasonable to me.

I learned that there was literature that was followed and sponsors guide sponsees in largely the same way they received guidance themselves.

The literature and the foundation of Twelve Step Fellowships are very important. I would learn to recite and quote the literature and so would Steve.

I read several books cover to cover aloud during the first several years of my recovery.

This is my experience working each step with my sponsor.

Step One: Honesty

Step One. We admitted we were powerless over alcohol — that our lives had become unmanageable.

> **"No trial has come to you but what is human. God is faithful and will not let you be tried beyond your strength; but with the trial he will also provide a way out, so that you may be able to bear it." (I Cor. 10:13)**

My sponsor had a few expectations that I agreed to honor. I was to send my sponsor a text every day listing three things that I was grateful for to cultivate a gratitude practice. The text was a group text with the other women being sponsored. I learned that these were my sobriety sisters.

I was to purchase specific literature and meet my sponsor for one hour every week consistently to read together. We read several books cover to cover.

I was to attend Twelve Step meetings, and I found great companionship with her and others. I felt love and belonging. I felt family. Consistently showing up at meetings eventually led to invitations to birthday celebrations, book clubs, holiday parties, events, and driving to different Twelve Step meetings together to celebrate each other's milestones and hear each other speak.

My first sponsor took me through the Twelve Steps. With every step, she asked me to read specific literature and to write responses to a few questions. Being the willful person I am, I searched on my own for templates to aid me in doing this "right". Millions of people have taken these steps before me, and I trust that other perfectionists also began with fear and trepidation of these step's unknown experience.

There was no syllabus I could see and no manual that I could familiarize myself with. I was following tradition, but I couldn't help but insert my own control into this process.

My sponsor was understanding, and I'm grateful for her showing me the patience and understanding I would need with myself through this journey.

My first assignment was to write down how my life had become unmanageable.

This is what I wrote and shared with my sponsor:

1. Have you seriously damaged your relationships with other people because of your addictive behaviors? If so, list the relationships and how you damaged them.

Yes. I seriously damaged my relationship with my husband. I seriously damaged my relationship with a sibling. In social acquaintances, I made people uncomfortable and had neighbors prefer not to be around me. My husband stopped wanting to take me places or bring people to our home.

2. If other people have told you how you have hurt them, then write down what they said.

Many examples go like this: Siblings and friends are angry with me when going out together and my not leaving a bar/club when they wanted to go and when I promised to leave. The more drunk I was, the more obnoxious and impossible I was when I felt there was interference in my fun. I verbally hurt people I cared about and put them into the position of babysitting me, cleaning up my vomit, keeping me safe, and they could not relax or have a good time around me.

3. Describe any missed appointments that resulted from your addictive behavior.

- *I missed picking up my daughter from school by falling asleep during the day.*
- *I was dizzy in church and felt I was going to pass out, so I walked out when I was scheduled to serve.*
- *At one employer's large event, I arrived a day early and drank in my hotel, missing an entire evening of team dinners. The next day, I missed team prep meetings and team/customer meals.*
- *At another employer, I was hung over many times coming into the office that I didn't get tasks done very well and, in the evening, passed on team outings to go to the hotel and drink more until I felt better.*
- *I was responsible for several church meetings to coordinate communications. I had canceled two in a row and made up excuses that it was about Arabella.*

4. Describe any times that you cannot recall how you got home.

- *I do remember getting to my home every night, but there were many nights I don't remember after seven or eight in the evening if I started to heavily drink at two or three in the afternoon. My children took several pictures of me slumped on the couch or in a chair passed out napping.*

- *Traveling outside of the home is where I wouldn't remember where I got bruises from or how I got from a team dinner back to the hotel.*

5. Describe times and ways that you have significantly neglected or damaged relationships with your loved ones to indulge in your addictive behaviors or because you were recovering from your addictive behaviors.

- *Out of guilt and resentment, I would cook, clean, offer sex to my husband, give nightly back scratches to the family, but I did not want to attend sporting events or school events. I stayed in the home office drinking and watching shows or reading books while drinking until bedtime.*
- *If I was invited to go on a walk, to the mall, to an event by my family, the answer was usually no from me because I wasn't bathed and would get defensive about needing more notice to get ready. I was overweight and embarrassed to be around people who knew me from before I had drank myself into such a state.*

6. Describe any illnesses that have resulted from your addictive behaviors.

- *I got the flu every year and colds frequently. I vomited at least four times a week for no apparent reason. I went back and forth between diarrhea and terrible constipation, which caused hemorrhoids. I bled out of my behind whenever I would go to the bathroom towards the past few months.*
- *My stomach was distended and I looked pregnant. It was painful to wear bras or to have my husband lie on me. I would feel claustrophobic.*

- *Memorial Day 2019, I passed out during the day from drinking and not eating. I had a seizure and hit my head on the door frame. When I came to, my husband urged me to crawl to bed. I didn't realize how bad things were because he had cleaned up a ton of blood. I passed out in bed and when I came to, I just said how badly my head hurt. We went to the emergency room a few days later. I would have needed stitches but the wound on the back of my head started to heal.*
- *I had insomnia and could only sleep three or four hours. I couldn't fall asleep without drinking until I passed out. I took naps every day and was completely exhausted all the time. I didn't eat regularly. Towards the end I drank all day, every day.*

7. If your addictive behavior contributed to excessive spending, describe the situations and why you did it.

- *I spent money on alcohol and hid the spending by getting vodka with groceries. I would hide the vodka bottle in the car if I happened to time a trip so desperately that he was home when I arrived with groceries. I usually did trips while my husband golfed or went to the gym. I spent about $50 a week on vodka.*
- *I spent money on a few programs for weight loss, which didn't work because it was alcohol that was making me gain weight.*
- *I spent money going to Denver to a transformation camp by a fitness guru I admired.*
- *I spent money on a popular point-driven meal plan.*
- *I spent money on a nutrition counselor for $50/hour.*
- *I spent money on a program to be a community college teacher. I paid $2,000 total for two classes and only attended the first few sessions before dropping out completely. I didn't bother asking for a refund.*

8. Describe times that you have withdrawn from social inter-action and isolated yourself to an extreme degree and why.

- *I stopped going dancing and to meals with friends. When I did meet friends to eat or travel and eat with coworkers, I had a hard time swallowing. I was very hungry but couldn't eat. I'd look at the menu ahead of time to choose food and when I got to a restaurant, the food looked very unappetizing. If I had enough to drink, I could eat.*
- *Many of my close friends had moved away. For the last year I wasn't working, I made no effort to contact friends. I left the house to go grocery shopping and attend church outings. I attended church every week and Catholic in Recovery every two weeks. I would occasionally go with Steve to his weekly men's coffee.*
- *I was drinking when I tore my calf muscle, so I stopped visiting with all of my fitness teacher friends and gym friends.*
- *I didn't want to even get out of the car to visit with other parents for school drop offs/pic ups.*
- *At sporting events I did attend, I was buzzed and sat by myself as I thought everyone was looking at how much weight I had gained.*

9. Describe incidents where you expressed inappropriate anger towards other people.

- *I had an ocean of resentment against my husband. I didn't stand up for myself, set boundaries and made him the villain of all my unhappiness – unless I was blaming my father. My husband wanted balance, health, and moderation and I didn't want that – I only wanted to drink. I would feel very angry with my husband and drank until I didn't care anymore.*

I unpleasantly spoke of my husband even after sobriety until working the steps and realizing my defects and denial and started to become accountable.

10. Describe embarrassing or humiliating incidents in your life. Were they related to your addictive behaviors? If so, how were they related?

- *Getting so drunk at bars/clubs I would fall or be dancing and lose my balance.*
- *Would run out of money and try to drink other people's drinks.*
- *Didn't get that drinking games weren't supposed to be where you drank the most.*
- *Several girls trips I would drink starting at six in the morning, so by lunch I would be passed out and miss dinners and had to be fed/watched.*
- *Stumbled around the neighborhood several dog walks and urinated on myself.*
- *Couldn't find my way around hotel lobbies and airports.*
- *Did toasts at weddings where I embarrassed the bride. Two different weddings.*
- *Cuddled with Cordelia when she was a toddler and threw up in her hair.*
- *Camping I drank and blacked out, but before I did, I was loud and obnoxious.*
- *Totaled my car.*
- *Was a nuisance at parties and interrupted people, made them uncomfortable, or made wives unhappy when talking to their husbands.*

11. Describe attempts that you have made in the past to control your addictive behaviors. How successful have they been? Do these

attempts show the powerlessness that you have over your addictive behaviors?

- *I tried to control my behaviors through food/weight programs several times.*
- *I tried to stick to only wine/sake.*
- *I tried to not drink in the house and only at restaurants. We ate out a lot during that time.*
- *I tried to drink only after five in the evening.*
- *Towards the end, I tried only to have two 750ml bottles of vodka a week, but I had to purchase at least three.*

12. Do you feel any remorse from the ways that you have acted in your life? If so, explain that in detail.

- *I feel a lot of remorse regarding how I disengaged completely from my family and marriage.*
- *I feel remorse for not trusting that God would keep me sober. And I feel remorse thinking that He could, but I wanted to continue drinking. I couldn't imagine life being enjoyable without alcohol.*

13. Describe any irrational or crazy set of events that have happened since you began your addictive behavior. Did you rationalize this behavior? If so, in what way?

- *I was very paranoid. I was anxious socially. I hid and lied. I would throw up and try to drink more afterwards only to throw up again and repeat the process. I would make excuses not to go on trips with family because I hadn't figured out how to hide alcohol. I rationalized that I needed help and it was physically unsafe to stop. I rationalized that my husband would not like the thought of AA or counseling, so I hid instead of being courageous for my own health.*

14. Have you avoided people because they did not share in or approve of your addictive behavior? If so, list these people and situations.

- *At work I would have a lot of disdain for people who didn't drink. I thought they were boring and didn't know how to live or let loose. I wanted to think they were judgy and frigid.*

15. Describe any dreams that you have had that exhibit the unmanageability or chaos of your life.

- *I had multiple dreams that I couldn't get enough alcohol and it was running out. I had multiple dreams that I was sneaking and getting caught. During the year before sobriety, I would wake up and be panicked trying to remember where I put my phone last, when I went to bed, if I hid my stash well enough, and look to see how many hours I slept.*

16. Can you pinpoint one time in your life when your life began to become extremely unmanageable? If so, describe that period and what was happening.

- *After I lost my job, I was completely depressed. I didn't sleep well, eat well, hydrate, or care for basic hygiene. I lost interest in my family and was going through the motions of the day until everyone went to bed and I could drink. I would feel most awake at about nine at night when my husband went to bed, and I could drink a lot without anyone questioning why I was so thirsty for the sports drinks or flavored drinks I was mixing with alcohol. I would sit at my computer pretending to look for work and I would apply for jobs, but I did the bare minimum to meet unemployment requirements. I would put hardly any effort forth knowing we had money in the bank and were not close to not paying bills.*

17. Is there one incident or insight that made you realize that your life was unmanageable? If so, describe it in detail.

- *Towards the end I think every day was unmanageable. Every day felt the same. I drank upon waking, all throughout the day, would nap, and drank all evening and all night. If I woke up at night, I would make myself a drink to get back to sleep. Unless I was asleep, I was consuming alcohol. Steadily consuming it all day every day for several years. When I was working, I would drink during the day yet get all my tasks completed. I had been doing this job a long time and put a lot in place when I was more sober. I had hired people who were helping with a lot of tasks, and they were smart, so they also helped with strategy.*

18. How would you summarize the powerlessness and unmanageability of your life in the face of your addiction?

- *I was not living for many years. I entered my graduate program in 2013 relatively healthy. I was an alcoholic but working hard at my full-time job, teaching Zumba, and going to grad school.*
- *The cohort was full of normal drinkers, so classes and study groups became drinking engagements. I would drink on the weekends during classes with several classmates. I was more than willing to be a part of this new habit for fifteen months. I really loved the cohort and had great friendships that I looked forward to throughout the week and the weekends.*

- *It was a real loss after that ended to go back to just being a mom and wife. I wanted to get a PhD because I didn't know what to do with my spare time. My husband suggested that I spend time with our family. I drank more and more instead. Very little brought me pleasure. Not being a mom and wife. Not working. Only church.*
- *I started working my last job before sobriety from 2015 to 2019 when my position was terminated. No exercise, no healthy habits, and self-isolation.*

FIVE-MINUTE REFLECTION: What are you powerless over? Is there something or someone in your life you have been trying to control? Is your life unmanageable?

Step Two: Hope

Step 2. Came to believe that a Power greater than ourselves could restore us to sanity.

"The LORD sets prisoners free." (Ps. 146:7)

I think I had the benefit of being raised Catholic, having knowledge of faithful practices, a relationship with the church, a Catholic immediate and extended family, and a knowing of a Power greater than myself.

What my sponsor asked of me for Step Two was to consider writing about my relationship to my Higher Power, how my Higher Power could keep me sober, and what led up to belief in my Higher Power. We also read through literature on Step Two together.

I was a little familiar with Step Two because for months I had been leading the Catholic in Recovery group. I had also begun to practice my faith more religiously and had received the Sacrament of Reconciliation. I spoke wholeheartedly at a retreat with a priest about my pain, my anger, and my fears. One penance I received two years prior was to work on my personal relationship with Jesus.

Before that penance I did not have a personal relationship with Jesus. I knew God the Father to be an Almighty Power, and I follow the traditions of the order of the Mass and received sacraments. I worshiped through singing, and through my high school bestie I learned about Christian songs and artists she loved. I remember driving to and from Silicon Valley for work and playing songs by Hillsong United over and over in the car and memorizing songs that really touched me, and I think in these ways I was reaching out for God.

One Christmas, my mom bought me a few religious statues, one of Jesus with his arms outstretched and one of Mary. I had those in my home office on the shelf, and in the evening when I would drink, I would look up at the statues and I would listen to the songs.

I would look up to Jesus. I looked up at Mary and prayed for help. I was reaching for God and He was showing me He was there, but it took the leap of faith into believing that God could not only restore my life to sanity, but take away the emotional craving, the physical craving, the mental craving, and obsession with alcohol.

It is my belief that no human power can help us in our addictions. The insanity is that we keep trying to save ourselves, help ourselves, and use willpower over and over. We do not have the power necessary to restore ourselves to sanity. We need a Higher Power.

FIVE-MINUTE REFLECTION: Can you come to believe that a Higher Power is more powerful than you in handling a difficult situation?

Step Three: Faith

Step Three. Made a decision to turn our will and our lives over to the care of God as we understood Him.

"For I know the plans that I have for you," declares the Lord, "plans for welfare and not for calamity to give you a future and a hope." (Jer. 29:11)

This step for me was one of the most important steps to make. To make this decision and commitment. In my heart and soul, I had made the decision to turn my will in my life over to God that night of desperation, and the next day is the result of being able to pour alcohol down the drain and not have had a sip of alcohol since then.

My sponsor and I read Step Three literature together and my assignment was to memorize the Third Step Prayer.

Memorizing was difficult.

My brain was completely mush from drinking for so many years, and it was a very difficult process to memorize a couple of paragraphs. I tried memorizing the prayer by writing it out. I got an app on my phone to help me with flashcards. I had a printout of the Third Step Prayer on my wall I would recite from.

There is one line in the prayer that stood out, and when I fully started to understand the Third Step Prayer it became one of the most important tools in my recovery journey.

This is the prayer.

> God, I offer myself to thee, to do with me, and build with me as Thou whilst. Relieve me of the bondage of self that I may better to do Thy will. Take away my difficulties, that victory over them may bear witness to those that I would help, of Thy power, Thy love, and Thy way of life. May I do Thy will always.

The key for me to comprehend this prayer and to memorize it was the part where it says, take away my difficulties, that victory over them may be a witness to those that I would help.

Those that I would help!

I have always been motivated to lead and help others. This was a call to me to be successful in recovery so I could help others. I understood the beginning was becoming willing to go through this process, and what the rest of the steps had in store for me, which were very scary and unknown.

But I was committed to letting God build me as he would. I am committed to helping others because God has helped me and I can show how this has been done in my life.

I became willing to become like clay and for God to mold me into the person He needs in this world for others.

I became willing to commit to recovery for the rest of my life, by the grace of God, one day at a time.

FIVE-MINUTE REFLECTION: Can you give yourself over to the loving care of a Higher Power?

Step Four: Courage

Step Four. Made a searching and fearless moral inventory of ourselves.

> **"Fear not, for I am with you; be not dismayed, for I am your God. I will strengthen you, I will help you, I will uphold you with my righteous right hand."** **(Isa. 41:10)**

Step Four took the longest to complete.

I had heard many times how much this part of step work would suck, and I had heard how many people stopped at this part, and I had heard many people talk about how long it took them.

I began to hear in Twelve Step meetings about people not completing this step and relapsing.

I did not think this step was going to be easy. That said, this step was a complete turning point and breakthrough in my life.

As with the other steps, I read Step Four literature with my sponsor. My sponsor gave me very simple steps to accomplish this, which was to get a sheet of paper or to use a Word document or an Excel spreadsheet and create a column.

In column one, I would list every person, principal, or institution that I was angry or pissed off at.

I would create a second column and I would write the cause of my anger or resentment from each entry in column one.

I would create a third column to identify from each of the column one entries what I felt was threatened. Some of the suggestions were that I had a resentment or anger with someone because my self-esteem was threatened or perhaps because my financial security, my sexuality, my physical safety, or something else was threatened.

I would finally create a fourth column and in this last column, I would turn inward and look at my part in any of these situations to see where I was at fault. I was to explore if I was selfish, dishonest, self-seeking, or any other areas where I was accountable to the situation.

Although the instructions were very simple, I found getting started very difficult. I procrastinated and I found ways to delay by searching "Fourth Step worksheets" online to see if there were examples or alternative ways to do this step. My perfectionism reared its head here because I wanted to complete my Fourth Step right. I came across a template relating to recovery and the steps, and I remember writing my sponsor a long essay answering these questions that she had never asked me to complete. My sponsor was kind to me and said, "Thank you, Jenny. Now please do what I've suggested you do." My sponsor patiently waited many weeks to complete my Fourth Step and we both knew that I was procrastinating. Eventually, I had to sit down and accomplish what she had asked.

I had several breakthroughs during this process.

The first breakthrough was about growing up. I had a huge hangup with my dad and the fact that he would not let me be a cheerleader in high school.

My friends and family know that I wanted nothing more than to be a solid Gold dancer when I was five years old. I love dancing! I loved ballet class, and I loved going to my cousins' cheer leading practices and learning all their cheers. When I got to high school, I loved watching cheer leading practice. Then I went home and memorized all the cheers. I would go to football games and study, watching the dancers and cheerleaders, and I wanted to be out there, and I wanted to be performing. I also wanted the attention.

I remember clearly reading what the guidelines were to become a cheerleader. I had to have a B average in school and I would need money. I knew my parents would not be able to afford cheer leading, so I got a work permit and job as soon as I legally could and started working at a sandwich shop. I saved money and I got all my grades up to what they needed to be. I then brought the paperwork home for my parents to sign to allow me to be a cheerleader. My dad looked at it and told me a few hours later that it said in the paperwork that he would be responsible for taking me to and from the games and practices, and he could not commit to that.

I remember being crushed. I was beyond crushed and held this against him for decades. I've probably told anyone within earshot for twenty years about how much I wanted to be a cheerleader and couldn't be a cheerleader.

From that point forward I was a disaster of a daughter. I worked more so I wouldn't have to be home. I was bitchy. I did not want to participate in family activities. I was angry. I thought everything about fitting in, being comfortable, being successful, and belonging was all hinging on that decision for me to be a cheerleader.

I isolated myself at school. I was shy and thought this was going to be the change in my life to make me belong. I was desperate to be popular, and I was more desperate for attention than ever.

Adding onto my resentment, when my younger brothers started to play football, I remember my dad taking off from work, offering to take them and all their friends to practice, buying pizza, and that just fueled my anger.

What Step Four did for me was for the very first time put myself in my dad's shoes. Young Jenny was a ball of curiosity. I wanted to experience things and I had no sense of self preservation. I was already boy crazy, finding dangerous ways to get attention and demonstrating poor judgment.

I'd been caught shoplifting with a friend. I had been caught talking on the phone and writing notes to boys about explicitly sexual things. I wrote a specific note at age twelve to a nineteen-year-old young man about letting him do to me what I had no experience about – just what I'd read about.

When I was thirteen years old, in the summer I was a freshman in high school, I remember meeting a sophomore. This sophomore boy walked me home and hung out in our court. I let him kiss me on my doorstep in front of all the neighbors, and my siblings, and my dad saw this through the keyhole so I could imagine his image of what Jenny the cheerleader was going to be like!

My dad was probably thinking little Jenny was going to be at parties, having sex, drinking, and drugging, and I'm sure all of that would have happened. At the time I hadn't done any of those things. All I could see was that my dad stood between me and popularity, belonging, and being just like everyone else.

There I was at forty-six years old and for the first time able to see, as a parent, his point of view. I was able to see his fear and worry for teenage Jenny. I was able to see that my parents did what they could to keep me safe. My parents went to great lengths to keep me safe. I had held that resentment for so long and I was finally able to let it go.

I've done a lot of work trying to understand little Jenny. I'm grateful for learning about my inner child and that she wanted to be seen. I'm grateful to learn about childhood traumas that little Jenny endured and contributed to some of these behaviors.

You may have noticed references to my body weight in this book. In my high school years, I suffered from anorexia. I have a long history of being unhappy about my body image, which led to very low self-esteem.

I'm grateful to see my mind, body, and soul in a beautiful light thanks to my journey.

I've learned to love little Jenny and love the woman she's grown to be. I'm grateful for God's love that has filled that endless pit of self-centeredness and need I had.

As I described to my sponsor one day the same things I've written here to you, my sponsor patiently and kindly described that when our needs are not met, we can often turn to unhealthy attention seeking. Well, there ya go!

Another breakthrough that I had was regarding my marriage. Neither of my grandmothers worked, and both of my grandmothers had very large families. I imagined I would be a stay-at-home mom and have a large family. I tried being a stay-at-home mom when Cordelia was born. I stayed home for nine months, and I almost went nuts. I tried to be what I thought I was supposed to be, and I pressed Steve for marriage and a family very soon after meeting him. I thought I was way behind schedule getting married at age twenty-five.

While home with Cordelia, Steve worked downtown and liked to ride his bike to work. He didn't care to ride home so I picked him up. Steve liked to be picked up on time, and one day I was behind schedule. I just got back from the grocery store and Cordelia was hungry. I was nursing Cordelia while wearing her in the mini baby carrier, holding on with one arm, bringing groceries into the house with the other arm, rushing so I could get in the car to pick up Steve downtown on time, and I thought, "No. No, I do not want this. I did not sign up for this. What was I thinking?!"

That was very early on in the marriage, and I was so disillusioned. I really wanted to be the perfect wife. I wanted to be the perfect mother. I had such an inferiority complex, did not know myself, did not know what I wanted, had no idea what real motherhood and marriage was going to look like. I was disillusioned, and the dream crashing down in my mind caused me to want to drink. I found it more fun to do laundry with a couple of shots in me. I found it more fun to cook dinner for everyone, with all their various needs met year after year after year, being buzzed. This is no excuse, but it was my excuse, and in my denial, I blamed that I was giving and giving without ever expressing what I wanted. I had trained everybody around me that I would always be of service and I would always put their needs first. I had trained everyone that I could be last, that I would happily clean up the dishes and plan the next meal, bring in the money, try to make the holidays work, and be fit. I had a terrible shit show in my head.

It wasn't until recovery that I was able to look at the situation and see my part.

I wasn't a victim of programming. I wasn't a victim in my household with my husband. I wasn't a victim of over-parenting my children.

The truth was that I was not willing to communicate my needs. I was not willing to love myself enough to say what I needed, accept, and comprehend that I could create a different life for myself. The marriage, our communication, our family, the entire family system was set up in this broken cycle, and I was training everyone how to treat me.

I looked at all the fear I had around the situation. The fear of being rejected. The fear of my wants being called selfish or self-seeking. I looked at wanting to be fit and beautiful for Steve because I held fear around my husband finding somebody else or being attracted to somebody else.

I had such an inferiority complex. My husband could tell me a thousand times I looked beautiful, but if I noticed him looking at another woman, I would think, "How can I change myself so that he will never look at another woman?"

Without going into every single personal resentment, you can get the idea of this process. What are we mad at? What caused us to be so mad and what was our part if any? All written down on paper, including my fears inventory, a sex inventory, a finances inventory, and my resentment inventory, led me to the next step with my sponsor.

FIVE-MINUTE REFLECTION: Do you have past memories that you relive over and over again, which cause you pain? Do you have regrets and remorse that you relive again and again? Do you have anyone in your life that you need to forgive?

Step Five - Integrity

Step Five. Admitted to God, to ourselves, and to another human being the exact nature of our wrongs.

"For where two or three are gathered in my name, I am there among them" (Matt. 18:20)

This step takes trusting in another person. I am grateful to have developed trust with my sponsor to complete this step. It was suggested that I read recovery literature around Step Five.

I had my notes from Step Four of my most secret thoughts and feelings.

When I was carrying around my paperwork, I completely imagined it was like a spy's briefcase and handcuffed to my wrist. I didn't want anyone to see my step work.

My sponsor suggested we meet for a meal, and we decided on a restaurant with big private booths.

Over the course of three hours and a lot of coffee, I went through all the things I had done. I went through all the things I had concealed. I shared my lies, my sins, my guilt, where I had been wronged, and where I felt I had been wrong to others.

My sponsor listened to me, and where there were areas of sexual abuse, incest, and trauma in my story, she was able to point out to me I was taking fault for things that were not my fault.

There were hurts where I was too young to have a part to be sorry for, and there were times where men were in a position of power over me and had taken advantage. My sponsor's understanding was very healing.

My sponsor could relate to the thought processes, the behaviors, the attention seeking ways, and the disillusionment. My sponsor listened and was understanding – she was not there to judge me. My sponsor was there to let me have a safe place to release all this pent-up anger, fear, anxiety, stress, guilt, shame, remorse, and regret.

When I had nothing left to share with her and my tears had dried, my sponsor gave me a big hug and suggested that I do what the Twelve Step literature suggests, which is to find a quiet place to pray, light a candle, thank my Higher Power, and forgive myself and others.

I knew more steps were to come, which were scary, but my sponsor reinforced we were only on Step Five. She applauded my willingness and said that I completed Step Five with courage. I was proud of myself for doing a good job on this very tough step.

FIVE-MINUTE REFLECTION: Can you tell God and another person the areas of your life that cause you pain? Do you reach for a distraction in alcohol, drugs, food, shopping, gambling, lust, or other unhealthy attachments to cope with what is bottled up inside?

Step Six: Willingness

Step Six. Were entirely ready to have God remove all these defects of character.

"Be sober and vigilant. Your opponent the devil is prowling around like a roaring lion looking for [someone] to devour. Resist him, steadfast in faith, knowing that your fellow believers throughout the world undergo the same sufferings." (I Pet. 5:8-9)

As usual, my sponsor suggested I read Twelve Step literature for this step. Several steps take a little less time to complete and this was one of them.

In Step Four, patterns of my behavior emerged so a list of what we call my character defects was developing. To supplement that list of character defects, my sponsor suggested that I list the seven deadly sins on an index card, and for the duration of one week, I was to carry the index card with me and make a tick mark when one of the sins came up.

I created my card with the list of lust, anger, greed, pride, envy, sloth, and gluttony and was ready to tick away.

Midway throughout the week, I sent a text to my sponsor saying that "Lust, pride, and anger were in the lead!"

Of course, I also did research and found many lists of character defects on the internet and added a few other character defect candidates to my list. If you research "character defects," you will find many lists and worksheets that have been developed over the decades.

I have found that every deadly sin has a heavenly virtue. Similarly every step in the Twelve Steps has a spiritual principle. Likewise, every character defect has a character asset.

This was the first exploration of who I was, and I began to form the concept of who I wanted to become. This step allowed me to realize the building blocks God would use to rebuild me as I had prayed in the *Third Step Prayer*, "God, I offer myself to build with me and do with me as Thou wilt...".

When my sponsor confirmed that my list was comprehensive and the index card actions were complete, so was my Step Six.

FIVE-MINUTE REFLECTION: What characteristics and behaviors would you like to change?

Step Seven: Humility

Step Seven. Humbly asked Him to remove our shortcomings.

For I will restore your health; I will heal your injuries—oracle of the LORD. "The outcast" they have called you, "whom no one looks for." (Jer. 30:17)

My sponsor asked me to do a few things for Step Seven. As you can guess, we read literature around this step. I also memorized another prayer called the Seventh Step Prayer.

This prayer took a couple of weeks to memorize as well, but I had memorized the Third Step Prayer, so I knew if I could memorize that one, I could memorize another.

My sponsor and I met together, and I recited the Seventh Step Prayer as well as said a prayer asking God to remove my shortcomings. I talked about my reflections about what this prayer means and about what this step means to me.

MY CREATOR, I AM NOW WILLING THAT YOU SHOULD HAVE ALL OF ME, GOOD AND BAD. I PRAY THAT YOU NOW REMOVE FROM ME EVERY SINGLE DEFECT OF CHARACTER WHICH STANDS IN THE WAY OF MY USEFULNESS TO YOU AND MY FELLOWS. GRANT ME STRENGTH, AS I GO OUT FROM HERE, TO DO YOUR BIDDING. AMEN.

I don't have any illusions or thoughts that God would immediately remove my character defects from me, the way that he removes the craving and obsession of alcohol from me, but I have found that I had to focus on these defects. It was going through this process that made me more aware on a date, a day, or week-to-week basis where these defects were showing up in my life. One of the simplest and most beautiful suggestions I received was to act as though and live, as though these defects of character had been removed. What a simple and beautiful way to start a new identity.

An example of this is I had a behavior of concealing. I concealed my thoughts, my desires, my insecurities, my feelings, my needs, my spending, and other behaviors. In recovery, I began to live honestly and be very intentional about sharing my feelings, my spending, my needs, and my feelings. I have found that changing my character trait or virtue through honest actions felt so good that it is not as though God waived His heavenly wand to take away dishonesty, but I took the actions of an honest person, and my character defect began to be removed as if He had waved a heavenly wand.

We want to make a change in ourselves and we begin to live and change our thinking patterns around this, so instead of, "I am an angry prideful person," act as though I was a person of love and acceptance and humility, and I try to practice the opposite of all of my character defects in my life.

FIVE-MINUTE REFLECTION: Do you accept yourself as you are? If there are values or virtues you would like to live more fully in, what is the first step to do that?

Step Eight: Justice

Step Eight. Made a list of all persons we had harmed, and became willing to make amends to them all.

"But he said to the woman, "Your faith has saved you; go in peace." (Luke 7:50)

When I got to this step, I had gained some humility and was willing to make a list, if it needed to be. I was willing to be honest and complete about who I had harmed.

The final list contained my closest friends. It contained the entire cohort from my Executive MBA program as they had to team with me, and I had not given my best during the fifteen months together. Of course, the list had my husband, my children, my mother, my siblings, my in-laws, colleagues, neighbors, and acquaintances.

I experienced fear around Step Nine and my sponsor led me first through the literature for the step, and one by one I received her guidance on who and how to make my amends. This was a very helpful process because I didn't feel alone, and there were a few situations where I would cause harm by offering an amendment and she helped me define those specific situations.

An example of where I could cause harm is where I was envious of another person. We'll call that person Sally. Sally might appear on my resentments list because I felt inferior to Sally and often thought bad thoughts about Sally, wishing I was more like her or being very unhappy when Sally was achieving success. In this case, I would not go up to Sally and say, "Hey Sally, I want to apologize for all of the bad thoughts I have had about you due to my envy." This action could cause Sally to feel bad about herself, take offense, or feel the need to take responsibility for my feelings somehow.

As with all of the steps, it is very important to become willing to make amends and make a complete list. It is also important to be willing to consider the wisdom of a sponsor before moving onto the next step.

FIVE-MINUTE REFLECTION: Do you owe anyone an apology? Do you owe anyone money or compensation from your past? Would it be healing to face this part of your past?

Step Nine: Forgiveness

Step Nine. Made direct amends to such people wherever possible, except when to do so would injure them or others.

"Just so, the Son of Man did not come to be served but to serve and to give his life as a ransom for many." **(Matt. 20:28)**

I felt more comfortable beginning Step Nine after completing Step Eight with my sponsor. Having a list and a clear set of objectives was helpful to me.

I love a good to do list.

I first did the "easy" amends where I had the most trust with people. I set up times to meet with my family and friends and had several lunch or coffee dates where I was open and expressed my alcoholism, my apologies for a situation where I made other people feel uncomfortable, where I knew that I had embarrassed them or they had to babysit me, and where I had worried them.

Overwhelmingly the responses were very loving, very gracious, praising God, and most people in my life had been praying for me for a long time. They had been praying for me a lot longer than I knew. They prayed for me to get help and to understand the terrible path I was on. I thought I was hiding my situation from everyone, and it was clear that I was not hiding from everyone. People who didn't know alcohol was the problem knew something was terribly wrong.

There were a few family members who did not want to meet with me, said they were not at all ready to go over amends with me, and as of writing of this book, those conversations still haven't taken place. I take peace in that I have followed the steps and I have been willing to make these amends. I have made myself available and keep the door open for an amend to take place, if the other person is willing,

Of course, the most difficult amends to make were to Steve, Arabella, and Cordelia.

That is where I had the most fear.

I had learned I could offer amends as living amends. I could offer to write a letter. I could offer to have a conversation.

I offered to Arabella, Would she like me to write her a letter? Would she like me to talk to her, or would she like me to never again be the way I was before and do living amends?

Arabella asked me to talk so we had a talk. I apologized for stepping on her foot when I was drunk on Halloween. For being too tipsy to swim with her so many times she asked me to swim in the pool, and I knew it would be unsafe to get in the water. I apologized for passing out and forgetting to pick her up from school a few times when I overslept. I apologized for all the things that I could think of. I think eventually Arabella got bored and she said, "OK mommy that's good." and gave me a big hug and our amends were complete.

Cordelia asked me to send her a text of all the things that I wanted to say in my amends and to use a lot of emojis. I sent Cordelia a text apologizing for the same things as Arabella but also specific things to Cordelia, like making plans with her and not remembering them and then being confusing to her as to why I couldn't make commitment after commitment. I apologized for the time I threw up in her hair and I took myself to bed to pass out. Cordelia sent me an "I love you mommy!" kind of message back and came out of her room to give me a big hug.

Stevie and I went on a walk. We were walking more frequently together, trying to be more comfortable being together in the same space and with this new knowledge of me being an alcoholic. I had hurt him badly with all the things I had lied about and that I didn't trust to ask for help sooner. Steve was learning about the disease of alcoholism and how warped my thinking was.

We were slowly building trust together. We were on one such walk when I told him the same thing I told the girls; that I could write him a long letter of what I was sorry for, we could have a discussion, or we could do living amends where I commit to being different and never being the same way I was before. Where I would never do the hurtful things I did with my Jekyll and Hyde character. Steve accepted that I could offer him a living amends.

It was by the grace of God that my husband and my children chose the ways they wanted to receive amends, and it's by the grace of God that forgiveness was in their hearts, and that God gave me the willingness to get this far in the Twelve Steps because I was utterly terrified.

I experienced healing in my relationships through this process of forgiveness and letting go. I had a long way to go to find self-love, but seeing the care for me in others' eyes was a beautiful start.

FIVE-MINUTE REFLECTION: Is forgiveness important to you? Why or why not? What do you need to forgive yourself for?

Step Ten: Discipline

Step Ten. Continued to take personal inventory and when we were wrong promptly admitted it.

The LORD's acts of mercy are not exhausted, his compassion is not spent. They are renewed each morning— great is your faithfulness! (Lam. 3:22-23)

I think Step Ten is a wonderful discipline of the Twelve Steps. It reminds me of the practice of an examination of conscience.

What I didn't want to do was have another buildup of anger, regret, and remorse and to keep reliving those negative feelings, which would trigger me to drink. I had worked too hard and been sober for several months.

After reading through the Tenth Step literature with my sponsor, she described the instructions to me and suggested I perform this step daily, preferably at night.

There are many apps that have been developed around the Twelve Steps and I found one specific to Step Ten. The app I found aligned to the questions my sponsor suggested I ask myself each evening such as:

- Was I resentful?
- Was I dishonest?
- Did I owe anyone an apology?
- Did I promptly admit when I was wrong?
- Was there anything I was keeping to myself that I should share with another person?
- Did I think today of what I could do for others?

It was very effective for me to develop this habit until I memorized the questions and could do it automatically in my head.

My family has gotten used to me blurting out all the time, "I owe you an amend. I am so very sorry for xyz."

I found myself examining my conscience frequently wanting to make repairs for any wrongdoings as soon as I became aware of them. If I thought I had poor behavior or acts of selfishness, self-centeredness, impulsiveness, or where I was unkind, I wanted to apologize immediately. It was a new way of living for all of us. It was much better.

FIVE-MINUTE REFLECTION: What two or three questions can you ask yourself at the end of a day as a daily reflection?

Step Eleven: Spirituality

Step Eleven. Sought through prayer and meditation to improve our conscious contact with God as we understood Him, praying only for knowledge of His will for us and the power to carry that out.

The LORD is my shepherd; there is nothing I lack. In green pastures he makes me lie down; to still waters he leads me; he restores my soul. He guides me along the right paths for the sake of his name. (Ps. 23.1-3)

Step Eleven is one of the most beautiful steps and brings me peace and joy increasingly every day.

Step Eleven is where I spend time journaling, asking for what I want and need, and surrendering to God the things that I need help with.

I've learned to practice letting things go where I offer up my fears; I meditate and ask what is God's will? I ask how I can be of service? How can I be closer to You? Am I serving my purpose and am I on the right track?

My Step Eleven practice has been just that – a practice.

I cherish the time that I can set aside to drink coffee, read books, read the Bible, journal, meditate, and really get in touch with my soul. I let my ego take a backseat, let God into the driver seat and spend some time praising Him, loving Him, and accepting and receiving His love.

Step Eleven has brought me closer to my Catholic faith, where I find in church I can close my eyes and be in God's loving presence. I also feel I am practicing this step when I am in nature and feel the sun on my face as it shines through the pine trees and beautiful blue South Carolina sky.

I have so much more to learn and the journey continues. I realize the love, abundance, the plan, friendships, community, and prosperity that God has in store for me has always been there.

I especially practice receiving God's love and mercy. He helps me feel worthy of it.

It has taken years for me to begin introducing myself as a Beloved daughter of God, and it is with certainty that I will continue this practice for the rest of my life.

FIVE-MINUTE REFLECTION: How can you draw closer to your Higher Power?

Step Twelve: Service

Step Twelve. Having had a spiritual awakening as a result of these steps, we tried to carry this message to others and to practice these principles in all of our affairs.

"Come after me, and I will make you fishers of men." (Mark 1:17)

As with all the other steps, I read through the suggested Step Twelve literature with my sponsor. I understood this step to be a step of servant leadership.

I experienced a transformation in recovery thus far by working the steps. I had been transformed by finally seeing my part in situations that made me unhappy. I was consistently making amends and had a commitment to living in a different way – with integrity.

I hold dear a list of principles, virtues, and values that I want to amplify.

I am close to my Higher Power.

I now, through tradition, can and should offer to others what was so freely offered to me – to take other women through the Twelve Steps.

I did find myself in the first few years in sobriety wondering what was wrong with me that I didn't have sponsees.

In my pride, I thought I'd make a great sponsor! God knew that He was going to move us from California to South Carolina, and I was not asked to be a sponsor until around the time we moved.

I enjoy the experience of practicing servant leadership, patience, and compassion with my sponsees. I also understand that alcoholism is deadly, so I try to instill the facts that we have a terminal illness that gets worse, never better.

Alcoholism is self-diagnosed and it is relentless in its pursuit to destroy us.

The Twelve Steps brought me closer to God, connection, love, belonging, peace, serenity, laughter, trust, integrity, and so much more.

Step Twelve is fulfilled when I volunteer at church, at Catholic in Recovery, and in Twelve Step groups. It is fulfilled when someone reaches out to me for help and I do my best to be of service.

I am called to share my experience, strength, and hope with you.

If you ever have any questions, you can reach out to me. I am also listing many resources at the end of this book.

Reflect & Write: Take a moment to journal about how this section resonates with you. What tools do you use, or can you use to develop a vision for your life?

FIVE-MINUTE REFLECTION: What benefits do you receive when you serve others?

CHAPTER NINE

PART V: What Life Is Like Now

The process of going through the Twelve Steps took several months. Throughout this time, I remained committed to meeting my sponsor regularly, completing my outpatient program, attending Twelve Step meetings, and facilitating Catholic in Recovery meetings. I was present and a better wife, mother, friend, and daughter of God.

In Twelve Step programs, people talk jokingly about the "get back problems". This is a phenomenon of things in your life you may have lost that you get back when in recovery. You can think of it like a country song in reverse where you get your marriage back, your dog back, your house back, your truck back, and your job back. I know, I'm corny!

For me, recovery was like that. I started to get things back in my life that were broken or lost.

I found a job six months into recovery working for one of the best employers and coolest companies on the planet.

I had made so many new friends in recovery and strengthened the relationships I already had established. I learned to detach from relationships that were unhealthy to me.

My friends were amazed and always considerate of whether I was okay being around alcohol. The first few social events where there was alcohol, I was hyper aware of it. It reminded me of a vampire series I read where the vampires could smell fairy blood from miles away. Ha!

My sponsor reminded me that God was keeping me sober at these events, and after all that I had been through, I had absolute faith that God was with me every moment and that He was more powerful than alcoholism. I kept doing my part and He not only kept me free from destruction but rained blessings upon me.

My marriage changed during this healing. I was beginning to love myself for perhaps the first time in my life. This transformation was changing me and changing my relationships.

Where Steve and I didn't know where we stood in the few months of sobriety, we had grown close again. At eleven months sober, we celebrated our twenty-first wedding anniversary. He asked me what I wanted to do to celebrate and I asked him to drive to the foothills to have lunch in the woods. I love being around pine trees. We sat at a little diner in Colfax, California, and stared at each other over lunch. Something passed between us and we had an unspoken affirmation that our marriage would continue. Where neither of us could see into the future less than a year before, God smiled upon us and we began anew. On the drive home after lunch that day, we began to revisit past conversations of travel we'd like to do, experiences we'd like to have, and we asked questions from the past like, "Did we think we'd like to get an RV someday?"

That Christmas, Steve bought me a wedding band, which we had never gotten around to in all our years of marriage. It was the absolute perfect gift and meant the world to me.

At this point, like a new butterfly I was spreading my wings. I saw that I was beginning a love affair with my life, with God, with my friends, and family.

My entrepreneurial spirit was waking up and rising with great force. My transformation started me on a path to find my purpose.

With the belief that if we have the willingness to go into the unknown, to take a leap of faith, to trust in God, we could all transform.

A question began to plague me: What was the blueprint for where I was supposed to go from here?

I have done a lot of reading, attended workshops, prayed, written to God, and asked what my purpose in life is? Of course, my self-doubts, perfectionism, and people pleasing have made this a lengthy and expensive process.

I have read, tentatively at first, about childhood trauma and the impacts trauma has on our minds, memories, and our bodies in adulthood.

What I have come to believe is that my purpose is to see myself and love myself as God sees me. To see my neighbor and love my neighbors as God sees them. To look at the talents and desires I have been given and offer them in service to God and His children.

It has taken years of soul searching to get to this point where I can write my purpose in a few sentences, and God brings me clarity the more I practice Step Eleven. It has taken a lot of training to tame the voice of doubt and judgment in my mind and tune into my heart and intuition. I am grateful for the allies on this journey and for God patiently waiting for me to sit still instead of running around like a maniac in my head.

I remember feeling like I had lost so much time; I had to catch up quickly. As though life is now a race and I have missed so much I need to sprint. Our culture doesn't help and as an entrepreneur, I am influenced by the hustle, give it all, don't quit, and "slay the day" mentality.

Learning new tools, journaling, meditation, reading the Word, praying, and surrendering have given me the space to contemplate a vision for myself.

I know it is hard to visualize being a different person or see yourself differently. I invite you to use the worksheet on the next page to get your imagination into action.

Every Day is a New Day
Worksheet

Wave a magic wand and visualize myself one year into the future. What are my goals?

What is holding me back from beginning the journey toward this new life?

Who can I call upon or seek out, or what can I begin to learn to help me move toward this new life?

Do I have the willingness to take a first step toward my new future?

What action can I take this week to move toward my new future?

The Word of God

I'd like to share with you some of the scripture that came to mind while writing this book and what it means to me. I suggest taking some time to look up each passage and ask God what He wants to communicate to you through His Word below. You are invited to use the space below my interpretation to write an interpretation of your own.

"Come after me, and I will make you fishers of men." *(Mark 1:17)*
Jenny, follow me and I will make your light shine to bring hope to others.

"The LORD sets prisoners free." (Ps. 146:7)
Jenny, I can set all prisoners of addiction free.

"For where two or three are gathered in my name, I am there among them." (Matt. 18:20)
Jenny, speak of me and bring me into your relationships. I am with you.

"For I know the plans that I have for you,' declares the Lord, 'plans for welfare and not for calamity to give you a future and a hope." (Jer. 29:11)

Jenny, don't strive so hard. I have a beautiful plan for you.

"The LORD is my shepherd; there is nothing I lack. In green pastures he makes me lie down; to still waters he leads me; he restores my soul. He guides me along the right paths for the sake of his name." (Ps. 23.1-3)

Jenny, I planned for your move to South Carolina where your soul would sing and you can further be my channel of peace.

"Fear not, for I am with you; be not dismayed, for I am your God. I will strengthen you, I will help you, I will uphold you with my righteous right hand." (Isa. 41:10)

Jenny, don't be afraid of the unknown and of what I am calling you to do.

"Just so, the Son of Man did not come to be served but to serve and to give his life as a ransom for many." (Matt. 20:28)

Jenny, follow my example and be of service to many.

"But he said to the woman, 'Your faith has saved you; go in peace.'" (Luke 7:50)

Jenny, your faith in Me keeps you sober and has saved you.

"For I will restore your health; I will heal your injuries—oracle of the LORD. "The outcast" they have called you, "whom no one looks for." (Jer. 30:17)

Jenny, share that I have healed you because the addicted feel outcast.

Answering The Summons

There is a song that I listen to several times a week. I am on a path to answer yes to this song through my thoughts, words, and deeds every day. This song also can be used as wonderful journal prompts. The song is *The Summons* by John L. Bell and Graham Maule.

Do you have a song that you aspire to live by? Can you meditate on the lyrics or use them as journal prompts and write your thoughts?

Twelve Step Resources

AA – Alcoholics Anonymous. https://www.aa.org/

ACA – Adult Children of Alcoholics, for those who were raised in alcoholic and other dysfunctional families. https://adultchildren.org/

Al-Anon/Alateen, for friends and families of alcoholics, associated with AA: https://al-anon.org/

CA – Cocaine Anonymous: https://ca.org/

CIR – Catholic in Recovery: https://www.catholicinrecovery.com

CLA – Clutterers Anonymous: https://clutterersanonymous.org/

CMA – Crystal Meth Anonymous https://www.crystalmeth.org/

Co-Anon, for friends and family of cocaine addicts, associated with Cocaine Anonymous https://co-anon.org/

CoDA – Co-Dependents Anonymous, for people working to end patterns of dysfunctional relationships and develop functional and healthy relationships https://coda.org/

COSLAA – CoSex and Love Addicts Anonymous, for friends and family of people with a sex or love addiction, associated with SLAA https://slaafws.org/

DA – Debtors Anonymous https://debtorsanonymous.org/

EA – Emotions Anonymous, for recovery from mental and emotional illness https://emotionsanonymous.org/

FA – Families Anonymous, for relatives and friends of addicts https://familiesanonymous.org/

FA – Food Addicts in Recovery Anonymous https://www.foodaddicts.org/

FAA – Food Addicts Anonymous https://faacanhelp.org/

GA – Gamblers Anonymous https://www.gamblersanonymous.org/

Gam-Anon/Gam-A-Teen, for friends and family members of problem gamblers https://www.gam-anon.org/

HA – Heroin Anonymous https://heroinanonymous.org/

LAA – Love Addicts Anonymous https://loveaddictsanonymous.org/

MA – Marijuana Anonymous https://marijuana-anonymous.org/

NA – Narcotics Anonymous https://www.narcotics.com/

Nar-Anon, for friends and family members of addicts https://www.nar-anon.org/

NicA – Nicotine Anonymous https://www.nicotine-anonymous.org/

OA – Overeaters Anonymous https://oa.org/

PA – Pills Anonymous, for recovery from prescription pill addiction https://www.pillsanonymous.org/

RA – Racists Anonymous http://rainternational.org/

SA – Sexaholics Anonymous https://www.sa.org/

SAA – Sex Addicts Anonymous https://saa-recovery.org/

SCA – Sexual Compulsives Anonymous https://sca-recovery.org/WP/

SIA – Survivors of Incest Anonymous https://siawso.org/

SLAA – Sex and Love Addicts Anonymous https://slaafws.org/

SRA – Sexual Recovery Anonymous https://sexualrecovery.org/

UA – Underearners Anonymous https://www.underearnersanonymous.org/

WA – Workaholics Anonymous https://workaholics-anonymous.org/

NOTES AND SOURCES

Alcoholics Anonymous World Services. *Alcoholics Anonymous Big Book*. 4th edition, 2002.

Alcoholics Anonymous World Services. *Twelve Steps and Twelve Traditions* (1989).

Bell, John L. *Will you come and follow me.* Tune: KELVIN-GROVE (Scottish).

Nakazawa DJ. *Childhood Disrupted: How Your Biography Becomes Your Biology, and How You Can Heal.* New York, NY: Atria Books, 2015.

Weeman, S. *The Twelve Steps and the Sacraments: A Catholic Journey through Recovery* (1st ed.). (2016). Ave Maria Press. https://catholicinrecovery.com/.

Wikipedia. List of twelve step groups. (Last edited on 6 March 2023, at 05:09 (UTC)) https://en.wikipedia.org/wiki/List_of_twelve-step_groups.

ABOUT THE AUTHOR

Jenny Teeters, MBA, is an author, certified health and life coach, certified Clarity Catalyst trainer, and devout Catholic based in the charming landscapes of South Carolina. With a heart dedicated to positivity, faith, and service, she has spent over thirty years in leadership positions in the dynamic world of high-tech corporate life. Alongside her professional journey, Jenny is a proud wife and mother of two daughters, finding joy in family life with her beloved lab, Hunter.

Jenny is committed to faith and personal growth, which has led her to become an international certified health and life coach, guiding individuals on their journeys toward holistic well-being. Drawing from her own experiences, she's embraced the transformative power of Twelve Step recovery, a path that has shaped both her personal and professional life.

Beyond the written word, Jenny is a dynamic speaker, trainer, and consultant, sharing insights on positive living, faith, and the importance of maintaining a growth mindset. Jenny's writing reflects the tapestry of her experiences, offering readers a blend of inspiration, practical wisdom, and faith.

CONNECT WITH JENNY ON SOCIAL MEDIA,
EXPLORE HER COACHING SERVICES, AND STAY
TUNED FOR UPCOMING PROJECTS.

Website: https://jennyteeters.com
Email: jenny@jennyteeters.com
Instagram: https://www.instagram.com/jennylteeters/
Facebook: https://www.facebook.com/jennylteeters
YouTube: https://youtube.com/@jennyteeters
Linkedin: https://www.linkedin.com/in/jennyteeters/

Every Day is a New Day Podcast on Spotify

Visit https://jennyteeters.com/gift for a free guided meditation.